JESUS CHRIST AND HISTORY

IVP Series in Contemporary Christian Thought

Christianity and Philosophy by Dr. Arthur F. Holmes, Director of Philosophy, Wheaton College

Emil Brunner: An Introduction to the Man and His Thought by Dr. Paul K. Jewett, Associate Professor of Systematic Theology, Fuller Theological Seminary

Christianity and Aesthetics by Dr. Clyde S. Kilby, Professor and Chairman, Department of English, Wheaton College

Christianity and Sex by Dr. Stuart Barton Babbage, Professor Elect of Christian Apologetics, Columbia Theological Seminary; Principal, Ridley College, Melbourne; formerly, Dean, St. Andrew's Cathedral, Sydney, and St. Paul's Cathedral, Melbourne

An Interpretation of Karl Barth by Dr. Kenneth S. Kantzer, Professor of Bible, Chairman of the Division of Bible and Philosophy, Wheaton College

If you wish, you may enter a subscription for the series, so that you may be sure to receive, on approval, each new booklet as it is published. Write Inter-Varsity Press, 1519 North Astor, Chicago 10, Illinois.

Jesus
Christ
and
History
by
George Eldon Ladd

Professor of Biblical Theology
Fuller Theological Seminary

Inter-Varsity Press • *Chicago 10*

Preface

ONLY a few decades ago the problems of history and eschatology might have seemed remote from each other. Eschatology was a final chapter in dogmatic theology which to many bore little relation to the actual march of historical events. Or it was a special development in the biblical world which could excite the detached and often cynical interest only of a few specialists. Or it was a preserve of Bible students whose historical interest lay in the "prophetic" interpretation of current events or the construction of a final chronology.

Today, however, the situation is very different. By a strange and fruitful interaction of theological development and actual historical events, the problem of eschatology has become a crucial one both for the Christian world and the world at large. The human story has been, and has had to be, reconsidered in an eschatological light.

Many forces and factors have combined to bring about this result. In the theological world, it is the product of a new and more genuinely historical study of the Bible, and of an accompanying criticism of the humanistic optimism which so often passed for Christianity prior to the first world war. In the world of historical development, it is the product of the catastrophic

[v

events of the century which have made nonsense of the Liberal reading of history and demanded a more authentic Christianity in place of "de-eschatologized" presentations.

The point is that both theology and life have put to us afresh, and in the acutest possible form, the problem of the meaning of history. They have put this question in such a way that, if we are to escape either the scepticism of futility or the illusion of Marxist apocalyptic, only an eschatological solution will suffice.

The gospel is this eschatological solution. This is the theme, and the significance, of the present book. This is why it merits the most urgent and diligent attention of readers. It opens up for us an eschatology which is evangelistic rather than esoteric. It claims us for the only truly biblical, and the only truly relevant, message of the reconciling action of God centered in Jesus Christ. It is indeed a tract for the times, concentrating the fruits of biblical and theological study and applying them to the needs of the hour, which are basically the needs of every human hour.

GEOFFREY W. BROMILEY
Professor of Church History
Fuller Theological Seminary

Contents

I. The Philosophy of History

THE PHILIPPIAN JAILER asked Paul, "What must I do to be saved?" (Acts 16:30). Today the question has assumed a new form: "Is there any salvation for the human race?" For modern man, the sense of being lost seldom focuses on the fear of losing heaven after death; it consists rather of a sense of the meaninglessness of present existence, of the emptiness of life. This feeling of personal futility is but the individual and personal expression of the loss of meaning in history as a whole. To many, living seems without significance because history itself appears to lack purpose and destiny.

What is the meaning and goal of history? No more important question can be asked today than that. The form of the contemporary question is a modern one. Outside of the Hebrew-Christian tradition, the ancient world ignored the issue. In ancient Semitic religions, the pagan gods were deities, known in and through the processes of nature and more or less identified with these processes. The great Greek thinkers sought for meaning in the realm of ideas rather than in the flow of history. Hesiod saw a process of degeneration in history from a golden to an iron age. Plato looked upon the course of time as a series of cycles, each of which begins through the activity of a creative absolute as a

[1

Golden Age and deteriorates under the hand of Fate; following its destruction, the absolute starts another cycle. Aristotle noted the circular movement of the firmament and concluded that the necessary coming-to-be of everything was a circular motion. Théo Preiss goes so far as to say that, with few exceptions, "all the known metaphysical systems imply or profess a cyclical vision of time" (*Life in Christ*, p. 63). The great Greek and Roman historians, Herodotus, Thucydides, Polybius, Livy, and Tacitus believed that the lessons of the past could give wisdom for the present; but none of them found a purpose or goal in history.

The Middle Ages were dominated by a Christian philosophy of history that stemmed from Augustine's *City of God*. This classic was Augustine's apology for the Catholic church standing over against the decaying Roman empire. These two great societies, the religious and the secular, were viewed as the city of God versus the city of men. The city of God, consisting of all true Christians, has its visible expression in the Catholic church, and is to be supreme over the city of men. In fact, Augustine interpreted the millennial rule of Christ in Revelation 20:4 as the present reign of Christ through the church in the world. Since the church was the medium of Christ's actual reign in the world, it must be supreme over all human institutions and demand submission of the city of men.

The rise of the modern scientific outlook rejected all attempts to understand history in terms of the Christian faith, insisting that the study of history should be approached with pure objectivity. The scientific study of history claimed one concern: to discover the facts as they actually happened, freed from dogmatic and ecclesiastical interpretations. However, such dedication to facts became itself an interpretation of history, for it demanded that truth must be sought elsewhere than in history. As Lessing put it, "The accidental truths of history can never become the proof of necessary truths of reason." Truth must be absolute and unchanging; history by definition has to do with the relative and the contingent. Therefore one must seek for truth in the sphere of reason or human spirit, not in the ceaseless flux of history.

Hegel attempted to understand all history in terms of mind or reason. The real is the rational, and mind is at work throughout the universe in an evolutionary development. Thus history is the history of mind or spirit unfolding itself through a rhythmic process of opposing forces which ever emerge into new syntheses. Karl Marx reversed Hegel's view of reality by making matter rather than mind or spirit the only reality; but he borrowed Hegel's dialectical principle of struggle between conflicting forces producing new syntheses to fashion a materialistic view of historical evolution, the goal of which is the dictatorship of the proletariat in a classless society.

In the nineteenth century especially in Germany, many Christian historians tried to apply a rigid scientific historical method to the study of the Bible. As a result, they found the truth of the gospel, not in the events or movement of history, but in the religious consciousness or in universal values. Adolf von Harnack

[3

interpreted Jesus as a prophet who taught the eternal ideals of the fatherhood of God, the brotherhood of man, the infinite value of the soul, and the ethic of love.

The most influential contemporary German theologian, Rudolf Bultmann, achieves a similar end by his existential interpretation of the gospel. Bultmann employs two different concepts of history: objective or positivistic history (*Historie*) and existential history (*Geschichte*). As an historian, Bultmann is one of the most radical of critics. Because the portrait of Jesus in the Gospels is that of a Divine Being, Bultmann concludes that the historical Jesus has been lost behind the mists of Christian faith. He thinks we can know almost nothing about the personality, consciousness, and life of Jesus. Furthermore, he prefers it this way, believing that the acts of God cannot be identified with objective historical events. By definition, God is the "wholly other" who can never allow himself or His acts to become the object of critical study or thought. God can be known only when He, as Subject, speaks to me. Therefore the redemptive acts of God can never become objective events of the past; they can be only present events of my existence.

Thus for Bultmann, the entire question of the meaning of history must be asked in existential terms. As a historian he states, "We cannot claim to know the end and goal of history. Therefore the question of meaning in history has become meaningless" (*History and Eschatology*, p. 120).

For Bultmann, the gospel is not something which

4]

God has done or will do in history; it is something God *does* in my present historicity. The cross of Christ means *my* death to my old life; His resurrection means *my* resurrection into the new life of authentic existence. Here alone can meaning be found—in the events of my historical existence (*Geschichte*).

Followers of Bultmann feel that he has gone too far in severing the existential encounter (*Geschichte*) from the historical Jesus (*Historie*). They are therefore now engaged in a new quest for the historical Jesus, using new concepts of history. They refer to Collingwood, who has argued that history has an outside and an inside. Objective positivistic history is concerned only with the outside. A deeper dimension belongs to the inside of events. Thus the thought expressed in an event is more important than the event itself, and the historian must seek to experience afresh the thoughts embodied in past events. Historical knowledge is the knowledge of what mind has done in the past, and the historian must try to reenact the past in his own mind. By the use of such concepts of history, the "post-Bultmannians" are trying to recover the historical Jesus, who will be relevant for modern faith, by discovering in him the same concept of existence which they find in the gospel.

In these modern interpretations of the gospel, whether Harnack's liberalism or Bultmann's existentialism, the second coming of Christ can play no possible role. Harnack considered such apocalyptic ideas to be the husk of Jesus' first-century Jewish environment,

[5

which the prophet of necessity used to convey the true kernel of the eternal gospel. Modern men must strip off the husk and preserve the gospel.

For the existential interpretation, the essential is alone that which happens in my existence. The nonessential includes all of the biblical accounts of the alleged objective acts of God in history, including the accounts of the incarnation, the resurrection, and the second coming of Christ. Such alleged events are mythological in character; therefore the gospel must be "demythologized"; i.e., it must be relieved of this burden of mythological acts of God, not simply by rejecting out of hand such concepts as did liberalism, but by seeking out the idea of existence which they reflect. By the use of this idea of existence, the gospel is preserved, freed from its first-century freight of mythology.

When we turn from this survey of modern ideas of history to the Bible's view of history, we must be struck by the fact that the Bible constantly looks both backward and forward. In the Old Testament Israel constantly looked backward to God's deliverance from bondage in Egypt; but she also looked forward to the coming of God's kingdom. The New Testament looks back to Christ's death and resurrection; but it also looks forward constantly to His second coming. The question which we must ask is, therefore, a twofold question: What is the Bible's view of history, and what is the meaning of the second coming of Christ in this historical perspective? Is the second coming of Christ essential or unessential in the biblical view? Underlying these questions is an even more profound question: What kind of a God is the God of the Bible? Is He the Lord of history who works in history, and who has a goal for history? Or is He a God who is known only as He speaks to individual men? The purpose of this little book is to set forth the biblical view of God and history and to expound the role of the second coming of Christ in this biblical perspective.

II. The Second Coming of Christ in Debate

APPROACHING THE SUBJECT of the Bible's view of the goal of history, we find biblical scholarship engaged in a lively debate about the meaning of the second coming of Christ. In fact, for the past fifty years New Testament theology has struggled to know what to do with the New Testament teaching of Christ's coming. We have already seen that the liberalism of scholars like Harnack was able to strip away such apocalyptic [1] notions with no sense of loss. Harnack felt that the kernel of the gospel could be safely preserved without the

---

[1] "Apocalyptic" is a technical term designating the kind of eschatology which conceives of God's kingdom as coming from outside of history, by a cosmic act of God that disrupts the present order and inaugurates the final perfect order. "Eschatology" is a more comprehensive term which includes all ideas about the final destiny of both the individual soul and the human race.

husks of eschatological concepts. Jesus was reduced to an ethical teacher compatible with nineteenth-century standards.

However, this idealized picture of Jesus was shattered by the work of Albert Schweitzer. Schweitzer is unquestionably one of the greatest minds and noblest humanitarians of our century. One of the areas of his fame is theology. He has given the world an interpretation of Jesus which has made it impossible to strip away the role of eschatology in his teaching, but he has done it in such a way as to undermine the confidence of many in the historical foundations of the Christian faith.

Schweitzer interprets Jesus, not as the incarnate Son of God, but as a Jewish apocalyptic preacher who came to his own people to warn them that God's judgment was about to fall, that the end of the world was about to take place, and that human history was about to be cut off in a great apocalyptic conflagration. Jesus conceived his mission to be that of proclaiming the imminent end of the world and rousing Israel to repentance to be ready for the coming kingdom. He did not come to tell men how to live in this world. He came only to warn them that time had run out and to prepare them for the imminent inbreaking of God's kingdom. This end did not occur. History did not end. The kingdom did not come. God did not act. Jesus died upon the cross with a plaintive cry of frustration and despair on his lips: "My God, my God, why hast thou forsaken me?" (Matthew 27:46). He was, in short, a deluded Jewish fanatic who died a martyr to his own

8]

fanciful delusions. Schweitzer concludes his famous study by saying that the historical Jesus, the man who actually lived and taught in Palestine, is of no help to modern man, but is an offense to modern religion because his views were completely alien to modern concepts of history.

Several theologians have attempted to meet this problem by reinterpreting eschatology, including the doctrine of Christ's second coming, in terms which would be acceptable and meaningful to twentieth-century man. C. H. Dodd has given us "Realized Eschatology." The gospel is indeed eschatological; eschatology, however, denotes not the last things but the ultimate things. Eschatology is concerned with religious finality, not with the temporal end. In the message, person, and work of Christ, all the Old Testament prophets' promises of a redeemed society are realized, but in radically reinterpreted form. The real meaning of eschatology is discovered in terms not of the future but of the eternal. The kingdom of God is not an order of existence which stands at the *end* of history; it lies altogether *beyond* history, *above* history, for it belongs to the eternal, not the temporal. It is the Absolute, the "wholly other." In the "eschatological" events of the gospel, the eternal has entered into the temporal; the "wholly other" has entered into time and space. The biblical terminology about the Son of Man sitting at the right hand of God and coming with the clouds is not meant to be taken literally. It is a symbolical way of describing suprasensible, suprahistorical realities, which in Christ have become available to men living in

[9

time and space. There can be no future "coming" of the Son of Man, for there is no before or after in the eternal order. Eternal realities cannot be confined in the categories of time.

An influential American theologian, Professor John Wick Bowman, has given us an interpretation of eschatology which he calls Prophetic Realism. God's kingdom is the rule of God in this world *on the plane of history*. This note resounds again and again. In Bowman's view, the apocalyptic perverts the biblical message, for it relegates the kingdom of God to a realm outside of or beyond history. He is equally critical of all neo-orthodox theologians whose view of revelation will not let them conceive of God working within history. Any theology which presents God as "wholly other," standing over against man rather than entering into dialogue with man, Bowman describes as "apocalyptic pessimism." Albert Schweitzer's altogether futuristic interpretation of eschatology is also "apocalyptic pessimism," for it, like neo-orthodoxy, cannot conceive of the kingdom of God on the plane of history. Schweitzer places the kingdom beyond history; neo-orthodoxy places it above history. Bowman places it within history.

Bowman's interpretation of the end of history is expressed in eloquent, almost poetic words. "There will be an end to history because its stage will be no more. The theater burns down; so the actors wrap themselves in their cloaks and go home! Home!—That is exactly where they do go. Home for the believer is where God is; home stands for fellowship with God." (*Prophetic*
10]

Realism and the Gospel, p. 270). This view needs no second coming of Christ. One day, human history will end, for the stage of history—the earth—will be no more. The redeemed will leave the earth to spend eternity with God. This sounds very much like a Greek concept of immortality.

The most influential continental reinterpretation of eschatology is that of Rudolf Bultmann. Although he has now completed his active teaching career, Bultmann's views are just beginning to make a strong impact on the English-speaking world. We have already seen that Bultmann considers eschatological ideas of the coming of Christ to establish his kingdom to be mythological and insists they must be "demythologized." To Bultmann, the term *eschatology* does not mean the final accomplishment of the will of God either at the end of or within human history. It designates, rather, the realization of the true meaning of personal human existence. Eschatology, which traditionally has dealt with the "last things" in terms of the human race, refers rather to that which has ultimate meaning for individual existence. In the eschatological experience of salvation, the individual is brought to the end of his old world and ushered into a new world that is one of complete openness to God. God is experienced in terms of one's own truest existence. As to the future of human history, Bultmann is agnostic (see p. 4). The second coming of Christ is not an event that gives meaning to the course of history. Meaning is to be found only within the individual's "eschatological" experience. The idea of a Heavenly Being coming to

[11

bring history to its end (the second coming of Christ) belongs to a mythological world view that modern man cannot accept. The truth embodied in this eschatological mythology must be reinterpreted in terms of individual eschatological experience. This process of reinterpreting biblical mythology is called "demythologizing."

When we turn to more orthodox theologians to ask about the meaning of the second coming of Christ and its role in the Bible's view of history, we are again dismayed by the diversity of interpretation.

The hope of Christ's coming has too often become a subject of controversy and debate within the church. Orthodox theologians frequently have been more concerned with the order of events that will attend the return of the Lord than with the fact itself and its role in the biblical view of history. Several different views may be identified. One of the oldest forms of eschatological expectation is found in Irenaeus (cir. A.D. 200), whose writings contain the first extensive extant interpretation of the Christian hope. The second coming of Christ will not bring about the immediate end of earthly existence. It will be followed by a final era of human history, when the kingdom of Christ will be manifested in the world for a thousand-year period before the final consummation. This so-called "millennial" [2] interpretation is based on Revelation 20, and the thousand-year reign of Christ with His saints in Revelation 20:4 is understood to refer to a literal period within human history after Christ's return. Only at the

[2] "Millennium" means a thousand years.

end of the millennium will the final consummation take place. Only then will death and evil be destroyed and the present order of existence replaced by a new heaven and a new earth. This view has come to be known as *premillennialism*, for it anticipates the return of Christ before His millennial kingdom.

A modern variant of this view interprets the millennial reign of Christ primarily in terms of Israel rather than the Church. This view is called *dispensationalism*. It holds that there are two peoples of God, Israel and the Church, through whom God is carrying out two different purposes. God's program for Israel is found in the Old Testament and is primarily earthly and theocratic. It is God's purpose to display His power and glory to the entire world through the destiny of the nation Israel. On the other hand, God's purpose for the Church is spiritual and redemptive. During the Church age, God has temporarily broken off His dealings with Israel and is forming the Church. But at the end of this "great parenthesis" when His purpose for the Church is complete, God will resume His dealings with Israel. The Jews will be restored to Palestine as a nation, the Old Testament cultic order of temple and sacrifices will be reconstituted, and Christ as the Davidic King of Israel will reign from Jerusalem over the world.

Premillennialism and dispensationalism are closely related but not synonymous terms. Dispensationalism is a variant form of premillennialism. All dispensationalists will be premillennialists, but many premillennialists are not dispensationalists. What may be called historic

[13

premillennialism understands the millennial age to be a further manifestation of the same redemptive kingdom of God now experienced by the Church, rather than a restoration of the Jewish order. There is therefore an important theological difference between dispensationalism and premillennialism.

Many theologians feel that biblical eschatology excludes any millennial period after the return of the Lord. His return will bring God's redemptive purposes immediately to their consummation, ushering in at once the eternal order of the new heaven and the new earth. This view is called *amillennialism* because it denies any literal millennial kingdom on earth. The "thousand years" when Christ reigns with His saints is a symbol of the Church age. The reign refers either to the working of Christ's kingdom in the world through His Church, or else to the reign of martyred believers in heaven during the Church age.

Another view postpones the second coming of Christ into the distant future. It expects the kingdom of God to be established in this world by the Church's proclamation of the redeeming gospel. The power of the gospel entrusted to the Church is able not only to save men, but also to transform the entire social order. It is therefore the mission of the Church, through the power resident in its supernatural redeeming gospel, to christianize the entire social order and usher in the golden age of God's kingdom before the coming of Christ. This view is called *postmillennialism,* because it postpones the return of Christ until after the "millennium" or the achievement of God's kingdom on earth.

14]

Because of such differences of interpretation, the truth of the Lord's return has often been a subject of controversy. These several views embody different philosophies of history. Postmillennialism expects the kingdom of God to be established by the Church's proclamation of the gospel. Dispensationalism expects the kingdom of God to include a restoration of Judaism. Premillennialism expects a realization of God's kingdom within history which amillennialism denies.

In the face of these several modern reinterpretations of history and eschatology, and in view of the great diversity of opinion even among conservative scholars, the thoughtful Christian must ask, What is the deeper meaning of the biblical teaching of the second coming of Christ? Is this hope as it appears in the New Testament merely a piece of Jewish mythological thinking? Did the early Christians simply derive certain elements of their world view or *Weltanschauung* from their religious environment of Jewish apocalyptic? Must the modern Christian try to disengage the essential meaning of the redemptive work of Christ from an alien Jewish eschatological setting? Or is there indeed a profound theology involved in the doctrine of the second coming of Christ that is essential to the biblical view of God and history? Furthermore, is there some central significance in the truth of the second coming of Christ that should be acceptable to all conservative Christians? It is the purpose of this brief study to show that the latter is the case, and that to eliminate the teaching of the second coming of Christ is to emasculate the biblical concept of history and redemption.

[15

III. The Biblical Presuppositions

THE MEANING of the second coming of Christ can be disclosed only in the context of the basic structure of the theology of the entire Bible. Underlying this doctrine are certain biblical presuppositions about the nature of God, man, and the world without which it cannot be fully understood.

First and most important is the biblical revelation of God. He is the living God who wills the blessing and redemption of man. He is the creating God who is the source of all life and blessing. God discloses His glory and goodness through His acts in nature. The stars in the sky, the alternation of the seasons, the return of seedtime and harvest, the fruitfulness of the earth, all reflect the faithfulness of God.

Modern man often thinks of "laws of nature" almost as though they were an unbreakable set of rules, which govern the forces of nature and to which God himself must conform. Such thinking is foreign to the Bible. The regularity of nature does not inhere in nature itself but in the God of nature. The "laws of nature" reflect merely the orderliness of God's activities in the world. But since He is indeed the Lord of nature, God

16]

can, if He chooses, vary His mode of action. He who initially created life can destroy life, and He can also recreate. The question of the "natural" versus the "supernatural," properly formulated, is not really a biblical question. It is a human question that often leaves God out of the picture and assumes that our observation of the ordinary functioning of nature is the measure of all reality. It is a man-centered question rather than a God-centered question; this reverses the biblical order. He who believes in the God revealed in the Scriptures, who is the Lord of nature, will recognize that what we call the "natural" and the "supernatural" in the Bible are nothing other than two different modes of the divine activity in the world.

The biblical view of nature is a corollary of its view of God. The world is God's world. We do not always realize how often our thinking is colored by the influence of Greek dualism, which finds a moral difference inherent in the realms of matter and spirit. Dualism thinks of the material as the realm of evil, the spiritual as the realm of good. Such dualistic thinking logically leads to an eschatology that finds ultimate redemption in the flight of man's soul or spirit from this fallen world to a different world, the realm of spiritual existence. In this view, the world, including bodily existence, is a necessary but temporary evil, destined ultimately to be sloughed off. Man will find his true redemption in an altogether different order of spiritual, i.e., nonmaterial, existence.

This again is unbiblical thinking. When God created the world, He saw that it was *good* (Genesis 1:31). The goodness of nature has indeed been marred by sin. "The whole creation has been groaning in travail together until now" (Romans 8:22). This fact, however, must not be interpreted to mean that creation has fallen from goodness to evil, so that it has become offensive to its Creator. *The world was created for God's glory* (Psalms 19:1); the ultimate goal and destiny of creation is to glorify and praise its Creator (Psalms 98:7–9). The world is not a temporary stage on which man acts out the drama of his mortal existence. Neither is it the realm of sin and evil from which man must be rescued. The world was and is God's world and therefore destined to play a role in the consummation of God's redemptive purpose.

The prophet expresses it in poetical terms: "The mountains and hills before you shall break forth into singing, and all the trees of the field shall clap their hands. Instead of the thorn shall come up the cypress; instead of the briar shall come up the myrtle; and it shall be to the Lord for a memorial, for an everlasting sign which shall not be cut off" (Isaiah 55:12–13). Paul employs more didactic language: "Creation itself will be set free from its bondage of decay and obtain the glorious liberty of the children of God" (Romans 8:21).

The biblical view of man is a second corollary to the biblical doctrine of God. Man shares with nature the fact of creaturehood. But man stands apart from all other creatures in that he was created in the image of God; therefore he enjoys a relationship to God different from that of all other creatures. However, this does not

18]

mean that man will ever transcend creaturehood. Indeed, the very root of sin is unwillingness to acknowledge the reality and implications of creaturehood. The fact that man is a physical creature in the world is not the measure of his sinfulness and, therefore, a state from which he must be delivered. In fact, the acceptance of his creaturehood, the confession of complete and utter dependence upon the Creator God, is essential to man's true existence. Man truly knows himself, recognizes his true self, only when he realizes that he is a creature. Then he accepts the humble role of one whose very life is contingent upon God's faithfulness and whose chief joy is to serve and worship his Creator. The root of sin is found in the intent of man to lift himself out of his creaturehood, to exalt himself above God, to refuse to give God the worship, praise, and obedience that are His due.

Salvation, therefore, does not mean deliverance from creaturehood; this creaturehood is an essential and permanent element of man's true being. For this reason, the Bible does not picture ultimate redemption in terms of escape from earthly, bodily existence. Salvation does not consist of freeing the soul from its engagement in the material world. On the contrary, ultimate redemption will involve the redemption of the whole man, body, soul, and spirit. The resurrection of the body is an integral part of the biblical hope. Redemption cannot be limited to the spiritual realm, i.e., to the realm of the human spirit. Since man is a unity, the whole man must be redeemed and his body as well as his soul delivered from the penalty of fallenness.

[19

The biblical view of history must also be understood in its relationship to biblical eschatology. The Hebrew-Christian faith is primarily an historical faith. Christian theology is not primarily a set of abstract theological truths or philosophical absolutes. It is the systematic structuring of the inspired meanings that interpret the redemptive acts of God in history.

God called Israel out of Egypt. He revealed himself as the Lord of nations and of history by His deliverances of His people within history. Through God's acts in history, Israel was to learn that the Lord was her God (Exodus 6:6–7). Yet God's purpose, even in the Old Testament, was larger than Israel. He promised Abraham, "By you all the families of the earth will be blessed" (Genesis 12:3). God chose Israel, not only because He was concerned to provide a way of salvation for individual men and for a single nation, but because He had a purpose for the entire race. The realization of this purpose will be the goal of history: the kingdom of God. God who chose Israel to be the people of His rule will finally extend this rule through and beyond Israel to the whole earth. When God's redemptive purpose is completed, "the earth shall be full of the knowledge of the Lord as the waters cover the sea" (Isaiah 11:9). The goal of redemption is never pictured in terms of the salvation of the individual soul, escaping to a remote heaven somewhere far off beyond the skies. The goal of redemption is historical and concerns men, not only as individuals but as a social group.

This concern for history is a unique element in the Hebrew faith in contrast to other Semitic religions. The

20]

pagan gods were not gods of history but nature deities, known in and through the processes of nature and more or less identified with these processes. The God of Israel was the Creator and Lord of nature—but He was to be known primarily in and through history. He was the Lord of history: His people were to enjoy His blessings in nature but even more in historical experience. Our modern feeling for movement and meaning in history, even in such a distorted form as that of dialectic materialism, is derived ultimately from the stimulus given to the Western mind by the Hebrew-Christian tradition.

In the New Testament, the people of God is the Church rather than Israel. However, Paul makes it clear in Romans 11 that the promises of God to Israel have not failed, and that Israel is yet to be brought back into God's redemptive purpose. Even though the Church, which is the new Israel, no longer has the national identity or political character of the old Israel, the concern for God's people in history is not surrendered. This is clearly disclosed by our Lord's eschatological prophecy in Matthew 24. While the forecast of the future of this age to its end says nothing about specific events or personalities and contains no mention of single nations or political movements, yet our Lord's concern is with history and with the fate of His people in their historical experience.

The purpose of this forecast of the course of the age is not to tell how to calculate the time of the end. In fact, Jesus warns against such calculations by saying, "You will hear of wars and rumors of wars . . . *but*

[21

the end is not yet" (Matthew 24:6). The Lord's discourse prepares His disciples for their historical mission in the world. This mission is not to build the kingdom of God or to transform this age so that it becomes the kingdom of God. They are indeed to preach the gospel of the kingdom in all the world (Matthew 24:14), and we may say that the kingdom of God works in the world through its emissaries. Yet an inevitable hostility exists between this age and the kingdom of God, and the disciples of the kingdom must be prepared to meet this hostility. The kingdom of God will not come until the end of the age, when the Son of Man comes in glory and power to overthrow evil and establish His kingdom.

Thus the end of the age and the coming of Christ will not conclude earthly social existence. The purpose of the glorious coming of the Son of Man will be to gather His elect from the four winds, from one end of heaven to the other (Matthew 24:31) into the kingdom of God. The kingdom of God remains in the New Testament the goal of history. Therefore we pray, "Thy kingdom come, thy will be done, on earth as it is in heaven." The New Testament as well as the Old is concerned with history and the relationship of God's kingdom to history.

A final biblical presupposition underlying eschatology is the nature of evil. God's kingdom cannot come until the enemies of His kingdom are destroyed. The final kingdom of God is the perfect realization of the rule of God, including the full enjoyment of divine fellowship and blessings by His creatures. In one sense

22]

of the word, of course, God's rule is omnipresent and eternal. His rule is intrinsic to His deity. "The Lord has established his throne in the heavens, and his kingdom rules over all" (Psalms 103:19). However, God in His sovereign mysterious wisdom has permitted His rule to be temporarily limited. He permitted man to exercise freedom and rebel against the Creator. He permitted sin to come into the world. In creation, God had displayed His goodness by making man the chief of all creatures and by subjecting the created world to man's care (Genesis 1:28), entrusting to him dominion over all other creatures. When man in proud self-assertion refused to accept the role of creaturehood, when he succumbed to the temptation to "be like God" (Genesis 3:5) and fell into sin, God placed the curse of death upon man and the burden of decay and evil upon the entire world, that man might be continually reminded of the fundamental fact that sin disrupts the enjoyment of the blessings of God, even in the physical realm. Life and blessing are God's gifts; death, toil, and pain are the toll of sin. The final redemption in the kingdom of God will include salvation from death, pain, and decay, not only in man's individual experience but in the entire created order.

Furthermore, the Bible reveals something about evil which even modern thinkers outside of the Christian tradition are realizing: evil is greater than man and greater than all men. Evil does not inhere in the nature of material reality. Evil, in fact, is essentially spiritual in character. The evils in the physical creation are but a reflection of evil in the spiritual realm. The root of sin

[23

is not in man's body but in his rebellious spirit. The ultimate source of evil, however, is not man but the spiritual world. The Bible represents this by its doctrine of Satan. Satan or the Devil is pictured as a spiritual being who has rebelled against God and who exerts every effort to frustrate God's purposes. Since man, too, is a spiritual being, even though he is also a part of the material created order, Satan is particularly concerned to frustrate God's loving purposes for man. That man may prove himself to be a responsible being, God has permitted Satan to challenge man with the dilemma of choosing between submission to the will of God and rebellion against it, by forsaking God for the lying enticements of Satan. Sin is essentially rebellion against God.

In this way, the Bible shows that evil is a power lying outside of man, a power which is greater than man, a power which man can resist but cannot conquer, a power which must be destroyed before God's kingdom can be perfectly realized among men.

Here are the foes of God's kingdom: Satan, evil, sin, death. Here are the foes of man's happiness and blessedness. Here are the forces which have doomed both individual experience and human history to a long record of violence, suffering, decay, and futility.

If these are the foes of God's kingdom, two facts are clear. Man by himself cannot establish the kingdom of God. The popular terminology about building the kingdom is quite unbiblical. The enemies of God's kingdom are greater than man and greater than all men. God alone can subdue them.

It follows also that human history, in and of itself, cannot produce the kingdom of God. Human history is a victim of the evils that plague men. History is the macrocosm of man; the awful tragedies of war, violence, oppression, and human exploitation reveal the sinfulness of the human heart writ large in historical terms. Yet there is something even more fearful than man's sinfulness. Behind and through human history lurks the dark form of an evil demonic power, before which even good men feel helpless.

Here are the presuppositions of redemptive history. God's kingdom must mean the redemption of all that man is, his physical as well as his spiritual being; for man's physical being is not foreign to his true being, but is essential in that it expresses his creaturehood. God's kingdom includes the redemption of the created order, for the world was created not to be the passing scene of one act of the human drama, but to glorify God. God's kingdom is the goal of redemptive history. It is concerned with mankind, not only with individual men. God must disclose His lordship both over nature and over history, by bringing His kingdom as the fulfillment and goal of historical earthly experience. Yet the kingdom of God is now frustrated by powers before which man ultimately is helpless. Man cannot rise above Satan, sin, and death to establish or to build the kingdom of God.

It follows, therefore, that only God can bring His kingdom. In the truest sense of the word, the kingdom is a reality only if God is God, only if God is the living God, only if God is the Conqueror of Satan, the De-

stroyer of sin, and the Victor over death. Only a supernatural God can bring His kingdom, and only a supernatural act of the living God can rout His enemies,
giving men the blessings of His reign.

This is the biblical background for the necessity of
the second coming of Christ. The second coming of
Christ means the inbreaking of the divine world into
the world of human history. Although it will occur
within history, there is a real sense in which the second
coming of Christ may not be called an "historical"
event in the technical use of that word. "History" in
the strict sense designates the flow of events, which
can be understood in terms of an unbroken nexus of
cause and effect, and interpreted in terms of analogy
with other historical events. The second coming of
Christ will not be an event arising out of history; nor
will it be the result of other historical events. It will be
a free act of God, breaking into history in the person
of the glorified Christ, to redeem history from the evils
of the centuries and to transform it into the kingdom of
God. It will be without real analogy. The incarnation
was indeed an invasion into history from God's world,
and so may seem partly analogous. But in the incarnation, the coming of God was veiled. Only the eye of
faith could behold His glory (John 1:14); even His own
friends thought Jesus was insane (Mark 3:21). The second coming of Christ will be a glorious inbreaking of
the power of God, by which God will do for history and
for mankind what neither history nor man can do for
themselves.

26]

IV. The Unfolding Biblical Perspective

THE RELATIONSHIP of eschatology to history can be understood only in the light of the nature of prophecy, as described by Peter: "And we have this prophetic word made more sure. You will do well to pay attention to this as to a lamp shining in a dark place" (II Peter 1:19). The prophetic word is here likened to a lamp whose purpose is to guide men through the darkness of this life "until the day dawns" at the return of our Lord. A Palestinian lamp gave a limited light. It was a small clay vessel filled with oil, which provided enough light to guide a traveler through dark streets, showing him loose stones or pitfalls which might lie in his path. It did not, however, illuminate the entire village nor turn the night into day, as modern street lights often transform our cities. The primary purpose of such a lamp was to guide the traveler along his way and to enable him to avoid stumbling or falling upon injury.

We would often like to change the biblical idiom and think of prophecy as a set of blueprints for the future. We would like to have every question answered, every problem solved. However, the prophetic word is a lamp, not a blueprint. It is given to guide us, not to satisfy our curiosity. It is important to understand that at any given time in the history of God's redemptive purpose, He has shed as much light upon the future as was necessary to guide His people in the present. At one point He would send one ray of light, at another time another ray of light. For this reason we find in the New Testament much more light upon the future than in the Old Testament; but we cannot appreciate the necessity and meaning of the second coming of Christ unless we interpret the New Testament teaching against its Old Testament background.

"Christ" is the Greek equivalent of the Old Testament "Messiah," which means "anointed one." The Old Testament itself contains no doctrine of a "second coming" of Messiah. It looks forward usually to a single great day of redemption, when God will intervene in human history to judge evil and to establish His kingdom. "For behold, the Lord is coming forth out of his place to punish the inhabitants of the earth for their iniquity" (Isaiah 26:21). "For behold, the Lord is coming forth out of his place, and will come down and tread upon the high places of the earth" (Micah 1:3). "I am coming to gather all nations and tongues; and they shall come and shall see my glory" (Isaiah 66:18). "For behold, the Lord will come in fire . . . for by fire will the Lord execute judgment" (Isaiah 66:15, 16). "And he will come to Zion as Redeemer, to those in Jacob who turn from transgression, says the Lord" (Isaiah 59:20). "Behold, the Lord God comes with might, and his arm rules for him; behold, his reward is with him, and his recompense before him. He will feed his flock

28]

JESUS CHRIST AND HISTORY

like a shepherd, he will gather the lambs in his arms"
(Isaiah 40:10–11). "Then the Lord your God will
come, and all the holy ones with him" (Zechariah
14:5).

None of these verses *in their Old Testament setting*
refer to the Messiah. They describe a final visitation of
God to judge the world and save His people. It is a
judgment in history, on the earth. The same God who
created the earth, who visited Israel in Egypt to save
them from bondage and oppression, will finally visit
the earth for both judgment and salvation. All these
verses speak of a coming of God rather than the Messiah.

This visitation is sometimes called the day of the
Lord. The Lord's day will be the day when the Lord
breaks down everything that lifts itself up against
Him, so that "the Lord alone will be exalted in that
day" (Isaiah 2:12, 17). The day of the Lord will be a
day of wrath and judgment against everything evil,
both among men and in the physical world (Zephaniah
1:7, 14, 18; 2:3).

Out of judgment will emerge the kingdom of God.
"In that day" Israel will be restored from bondage
(Amos 9:11). "In that day" God's dispersed people will
be regathered, and the Lord will reign over them forever (Micah 4:7). "In that day" all weapons of war
and all instruments of evil will be swept away (Micah
5:10 ff.). "In that day" the curse will be lifted. The earth
will become fruitful, the deaf will hear, the blind will
see, and the poor will rejoice in the Lord (Isaiah
29:18–19).

[29

When God visits His people to redeem them, He will raise up a messianic King to rule over them and to execute justice and righteousness (Isaiah 11:4). Violence and evil will be purged from the earth, and "the earth shall be full of the knowledge of the Lord as the waters cover the sea" (vss. 6–9). All this will happen because "In that day the root of Jesse [the messianic King] shall stand as an ensign to the peoples; him shall the nations seek, and his dwelling shall be glorious" (vs. 10). In this future kingdom, God's people will be gathered in righteousness and blessing. God will make a new covenant with them, when He will give them a new heart and a new spirit, that they may be perfectly obedient to their God (Jeremiah 31:33–34; Ezekiel 36:25–27). He will forgive their sins and will pour His Spirit upon all His people (Joel 2:28). He will open a fountain to cleanse them from all uncleanness (Zechariah 13:1). God will be their God and they will be His people (Jeremiah 31:33), and God will dwell in their midst (Zechariah 2:10–11).

In addition to the expectation of a messianic King, two other messianic portraits appear in the Old Testament which are not integrated with the prophecies of the messianic King. In Isaiah 53, the Servant of the Lord pursues a path of meekness and suffering, and finally pours out His soul in death to bear the sin of the people and to make atonement for the transgressors. This suffering Servant is not, in the Old Testament, identified with the messianic King; and Jewish theology could never quite decide what to do with this prophecy.

There is an entirely different portrait in Daniel 7. In

30]

this vision "one like a son of man" comes to the Ancient of Days, and to Him is given the kingdom of God that all the peoples, nations, and languages should serve Him in an everlasting dominion and rule which shall never pass away (Daniel 7:13–14). He is an individual who represents and is identified with the people of God (vs. 18). However, this heavenly Son of Man is not identified with the messianic King; and neither Son of Man nor Messiah is identified with the suffering Servant. The relationship of these several prophecies was never understood until our Lord came to fulfill them. This is why we cannot understand the Old Testament apart from its New Testament fulfillment. From the Old Testament alone, one would think that these were three different personages, each with a separate mission.

The Old Testament neither shows the relationship existing among these three messianic personages nor outlines a program of events by which God's kingdom is to be established. Yet several important features characterize the kingdom of God, and these must not be overlooked.

The kingdom is a kingdom in history. It primarily concerns, not the salvation of the individual soul, but the salvation of God's people. It will mean the consummation of God's redemptive working with Israel in history. The God who saved Israel from the bondage of Egypt will finally save His people from bondage to all sin and evil.

The kingdom is a kingdom produced, not by history, but by God. But the Old Testament does not conceive of all history as a manifestation of God's power working

[31

redemptively in all historical processes. On the contrary, there is an evil element, a demonic force at work in history which causes men and nations to exalt themselves against God and oppose His holy will. Therefore God became uniquely active in one stream of history—in the experience of Israel—to change the course of history and to bring to pass His purposes for all men. Israel escaped from Egypt, not because she successfully revolted against the Egyptians or because of Moses' wisdom and cunning. God acted and delivered Israel from Egypt. The final deliverance from evil in the kingdom of God will be caused only by a final and mighty act of God, when all evil is destroyed and God's people saved.

The kingdom of God will be both spiritual and material. There is no purely "spiritual" salvation. Sin has cursed man in his relationship to God, in his relationship to his fellowmen, in his relationship to himself, and even in his relationship to his physical environment. Therefore salvation must involve deliverance from *all* evil. Only a mighty visitation of God in judgment, only a new creative act of God who is Lord of both nature and history, can avail to rescue men from all that evil signifies. This divine act of salvation is viewed in the Old Testament as a single great redemptive event, which will take place on the day of the Lord.

The New Testament further unfolds God's redemptive purpose, revealing its fulfillment as far more complex than the Old Testament prophecies suggest. However, a redemption that is both spiritual and material in the Old Testament does not become exclusively spiritual in the New. Redemption of the physical order remains a continuing feature in the New Testament (Romans 8:21). But *the redemptive event, which was viewed as one day in the Old Testament, in the New Testament is seen as two days.* The single redemptive act expected at the day of the Lord has now become two acts. These two acts are the incarnation of Christ and His second coming.

This does not imply that God has changed His plans, or that the Old Testament is in error. It merely indicates that in the movement of redemptive history, God progressively revealed the steps by which He will accomplish His purposes for man's redemption. There are in the New Testament, as it were, two days of redemption. The coming of Christ in history ushered in the fulfillment of the Old Testament promise of salvation; yet the second coming of Christ must occur to bring this salvation to its consummation.

This is why the New Testament redemption involves a strange tension between present fulfillment and future consummation. In the synagogue at Nazareth our Lord read a passage from Isaiah which foretold the "year of the Lord's favor," i.e., the coming of the kingdom of God; and then he announced, "Today this scripture has been fulfilled in your hearing" (Luke 4:21). Yet the prophecy in Isaiah announced "the day of vengeance of our God" (Isaiah 61:2), but Jesus did not include these words in His proclamation of fulfillment. The day of the Lord's favor has come, but the day of God's vengeance stands yet in the future.

This tension between fulfillment and consummation

[33

is the reason the New Testament speaks of the great redemptive realities as something both present and future. Thus Paul can say, "Behold, now is the acceptable time; behold, now is the day of salvation" (II Corinthians 6:2); yet Peter speaks of "a salvation ready to be revealed in the last time" (I Peter 1:5). Thus we are told that the kingdom of God has come (Matthew 12:28; Luke 17:21); yet we pray for its coming (Matthew 6:10). Thus we have eternal life as a present possession (John 3:36; 10:10); yet we shall receive eternal life in the future (John 12:25; Matthew 25:46).

The gospel proclaimed in the New Testament is the good news that "the Lord God of Israel . . . has visited and redeemed his people" (Luke 1:68). It is the proclamation of what God *has done* in history in Jesus Christ. Yet everywhere in the New Testament the day of the Lord remains, as in the Old Testament, a future day of eschatological consummation (I Thessalonians 5:2; I Corinthians 1:8; II Thessalonians 2:2).

We may change the metaphor by saying that in the Old Testament the drama of salvation occurs in one great act, while in the New Testament it has become two acts. But it is the same play. This means that *the second coming of Christ does not stand in the future by itself, but is rather inseparable from His past work in history.* Incarnation, second coming: these are the two steps in the accomplishment of the messianic redemption. Together they constitute a single event.

This fact can be illustrated in two ways, by a consideration of Jesus' messianic office and a consideration of His messianic work.

The New Testament shows us that the three messianic portraits in the Old Testament—those of suffering Servant, messianic King, and Son of Man—depict different aspects of the one messianic personage. This is made clear by our Lord's use of the term *Son of Man,* which is quite different from the Old Testament use.

In Daniel, the Son of Man is associated with a dramatic "apocalyptic" inbreaking of God's kingdom. This coming of God's kingdom is first described in Daniel in Nebuchadnezzar's dream of a great image that represented the several successive empires of world history. Nebuchadnezzar saw a stone, cut out by no human hand, smite the image on its feet, breaking the image and grinding it to powder so that the wind swept it away. Then the stone which smote the image grew until it became a mountain and filled the whole earth (Daniel 2:31–35). The message of this dream was that the kingdom of God would not arise gradually within history by a slow process of growth or evolution, but would come suddenly, catastrophically by a mighty act of God to accomplish both judgment and salvation. The kingdom of God would come in history, but it would come from outside of history.

In the parallel vision in the seventh chapter we are told that this kingdom will be given to the Son of Man, who will come with the clouds of heaven and will then rule in His kingdom over all nations on the earth forever (Daniel 7:13–14).

Jesus taught that He was the Son of Man who one day will come with the clouds and with power and great glory, as Daniel described, to establish the kingdom of

[35

God (Matthew 16:27; 24:27; 25:31; 13:41). But first, *before He appears in power and glory, the Son of Man has appeared humbly on earth to fulfill a mission of suffering and death*. The Son of Man has a twofold mission: present suffering and future glory.

Even in His humility, He is the Son of Man. As this Son of Man from heaven, He has authority on earth to forgive sins (Mark 2:10). He is Lord of the sabbath and has authority to reinterpret the Law of Moses (Mark 2:28). He is indeed the channel of communication between heaven and earth (John 1:51). Yet even though He is the heavenly Son of Man, He is among men in weakness, without a home (Matthew 8:20), destined to be surrendered into the hands of men (Matthew 17:22), to be tortured and finally put to death (Matthew 20:18–19). This, however, was no historical accident; it was the *mission* of the Son of Man to come to give His life a ransom for many (Matthew 20:28). Suffering and death were to be His present mission, glory and exaltation as the Judge of the world His future destiny. As the Son of Man on earth, He must first fulfill the role of the suffering Servant. A second phase of His redemptive mission is His future coming in glory.

This twofold mission of suffering and of glory are not two unrelated acts; rather, they are two phases of a single redemptive work. This is shown by such sayings as Mark 8:38: "For whoever is ashamed of me and of my words in this adulterous and sinful generation, of him will the Son of Man also be ashamed, when he comes in the glory of his Father with the holy angels."

36]

The response of men to the humble, suffering Son of Man will determine their judgment by the glorious Son of Man. He is the same Son of Man in suffering and in glory. As men confess Him in His atoning sufferings, He will confess them in His glory.

Thus it becomes clear that before the Son of Man comes in glory to judge the world, to purge the earth of all evil, and to gather the righteous into the kingdom of God (Matthew 13:37–43), He has a prior mission to fulfill: that of suffering and death. The suffering Servant of Isaiah 53 is indeed the Son of Man of Daniel 7; but His mission of suffering and death must precede and provide the basis for His mission as the heavenly Son of Man.

This twofold drama of salvation is illustrated, not only by Jesus' messianic office but also by His messianic work. We have seen that the Old Testament looks forward to a single great day of the Lord, when God will intervene in history to destroy evil and to gather His people into the kingdom of God. The further revelation in the New Testament shows us something that God did not disclose in the Old Testament: the triumph of God's kingdom over evil occurs in two acts, not one.

The New Testament teaches that the two greatest enemies of God's kingdom are death and Satan. The purpose of Jesus' total redemptive mission is summed up concisely in I Corinthians 15:25–26: "For he must reign until he has put all his enemies under his feet. The last enemy to be destroyed is death." Here is the

[37

final goal of Jesus' redemptive work: to deliver "the kingdom to God the Father after destroying every rule and every authority and power" (vs. 24).

This conquest of God's kingdom occurs in at least two acts. The death of Jesus of Nazareth was not merely the death of a man. He was the heavenly Son of Man on earth who came to grapple with death and to destroy it. Dying was His very mission (Mark 10:45). Through His death and resurrection, He "abolished death and brought life and immortality to light through the gospel" (II Timothy 1:10).

Here is an amazing statement. Death has already been abolished! Obviously, this verse requires explanation. The Greek word translated "abolished" is the same word translated "destroy" in I Corinthians 15:26. It can mean "to destroy," but it can also mean "to break the power, to make ineffective." The destruction of death occurs in two acts. By His death and resurrection Christ has already attacked the enemy, death. He has already broken its power. He has already brought to men the blessing of the eternal life of the future kingdom of God.

This is why Paul describes the resurrection of Jesus Christ as the beginning of the final resurrection (I Corinthians 15:23). The resurrection of Jesus was not the reanimation of a dead body to physical life. Lazarus had been restored from death to physical life (John 11:44), but Lazarus never dreamed of saying, "I am the resurrection and the life; because I live, you shall live also." Lazarus was a mortal man who was restored to mortal life.

Not so with Jesus' resurrection! His resurrection denotes something new, something never before experienced. It demonstrated the emergence of a new order of life, resurrection life, the life of the kingdom of God. It may be crudely described in these words: a piece of the resurrection of the last day, which will introduce the eschatological kingdom of God, has been split off and implanted in the midst of human history. The eschatological resurrection has already begun. Therefore the Christian hope of resurrection and immortality is far more than a hope; it is a certainty based on the fact that the first stage of the resurrection has already occurred. We merely await the second stage of the event.

This is the meaning of eternal life. It is the life of the future eschatological kingdom of God (Matthew 19:16, 23). Yet this life is already ours through the resurrection of Christ. He brought into human history the life and immortality of the kingdom of God. We may therefore even now experience His resurrection life (Ephesians 2:5; Romans 6:4). This is why the Gospel of John says so much about eternal life as a present reality (John 3:36; 10:10). The life of the resurrection (John 5:29) has become present experience (5:25) because the Bearer of eternal life (5:26) and the Conqueror of death (11:25–26) has come among men.

Nevertheless, we die. Although we have eternal life, we go to the grave. The mortician who prepares a corpse for burial is unconcerned whether the deceased was Christian or non-Christian. In either case, the body is dead.

The present victory of Christ over death is a real vic-

[39

tory, but it is only a partial victory. Death must be finally destroyed so that God's people no longer die. Mortality must be swallowed up by life (II Corinthians 5:4). This final victory will occur only at the end of Christ's reign. Man cannot conquer death; medical and biological science cannot conquer death. Only the Son of God, who has already conquered death, can finally destroy it. Therefore Christ must come again to consummate the victory He has already won. At the end, death and the grave are to be thrown into the lake of fire (Revelation 20:14). Apart from the second coming of Christ, God's victory over death remains incomplete. The conquest is unfinished, the triumph only provisional. But His coming is assured, because He will certainly finish what He has begun. He came once to break the power of death; He will come again to destroy death forever.

A second enemy to be destroyed is evil and the spiritual source of evil—Satan. The Gospels tell us that at the heart of our Lord's earthly ministry was a struggle with satanic evil. Satan assaulted Jesus in the wilderness and tried to turn Him aside from His God-appointed mission. Satan tried to entice Jesus to take a short-cut to His destiny as glorious Son of Man by avoiding the cross. He urged Jesus to compel recognition of His glory by spectacular miracles. He promised to install Jesus as Lord of the world if Jesus would heed him (Matthew 4:5–10).

Jesus in turn described His own mission as an assault against the kingdom of Satan. One of His most characteristic and repeated miracles was the exorcism of de-

40]

mons. Everywhere He went, Jesus delivered men from this satanic bondage. Mark sounds this note as one of the most significant aspects of His ministry. The people said, "What is this? A new teaching! With authority he commands even the unclean spirits, and they obey him" (Mark 1:27).

When the Pharisees accused Him of being in league with Satan himself, Jesus replied that the charge was ridiculous, for it would entail civil war within Satan's household, and the fall of his kingdom (Matthew 12:25–26). Then Jesus spoke these significant words: "Or how can one enter a strong man's house and plunder his goods, unless he first binds the strong man? Then indeed he may plunder his house" (Matthew 12:29).

Satan is the strong man. His "goods" are men and women—human personalities—in bondage to satanic powers, to evil. While demon possession is the most extreme manifestation of satanic power, it is exercised only over a few men. Paul tells us that the heart of satanic evil is bondage to darkness, blindness to the glory of God (II Corinthians 4:4). Jesus' mission was to deliver men from the dominion of darkness and transfer them to the rule of God (Colossians 1:13). However, first He must defeat the strong man. Jesus cannot enter Satan's house and plunder his goods, delivering men from bondage to darkness, except He *"first* binds the strong man."

Jesus has already attacked Satan's kingdom. He has assaulted his house. He has already "bound" the strong man. Because this victory over satanic evil has been

[41

won, we may now experience deliverance from darkness in the freedom of Christ's kingdom.

Hebrews expresses this same truth in different language. Since those whom Christ would redeem are flesh and blood, He, the heavenly Son of Man, took upon Him the same human form and nature, "that through death he might destroy him who has the power of death, that is, the devil, and deliver all ·those who through fear of death were subject to lifelong bondage" (Hebrews 2:14–15). The death of Jesus, as well as His life and miracles, was an attack on Satan. Through His death, Jesus has assaulted and "destroyed" him who has the power of death. This word "destroy" is the same word we have already met in I Corinthians 15:24 and II Timothy 1:10. It means "to break the power." Christ, both by His life and death, has broken Satan's power, has "bound" him. God's kingdom has assaulted Satan's kingdom and won a great victory. Satan is now, because of the incarnation, a defeated foe.

Yet evil remains in the world. To be sure, there is far more righteousness in human history than before Christ came. The gospel of Jesus' incarnation, death, and resurrection does far more than promise a blessed future to the individual soul. The gospel changes lives. It revolutionizes human personalities. It transforms human conduct. It rebuilds homes and communities, and sometimes even nations. No Christian missionary is content to preach a spiritual salvation to primitive people while leaving their bodies and minds in bondage to filth, disease, superstition, and ignorance. Wherever it goes, the gospel has power to transform all life to-

42]

ward righteousness, delivering men from bondage to evil of all kinds.

Yet the world continues to be an evil place. The kingdom of God has come into history and is at work in history. Nevertheless, history has not become the kingdom of God. Today many of our best minds who do not accept the distinctly Christian teaching recognize a demonic element in human history. Evil is greater than man and greater than all men; and our generation is fearful that evil may destroy it.

The second coming of Christ is necessary to complete the conquest of evil. This man cannot do; only God can conquer and destroy Satan. We may picture the conquest of evil as a warfare with two great battles. In His incarnation, Christ attacked Satan and won a mighty victory. He saw Satan fall from his place of power in heaven (Luke 10:18). The warfare has been launched; the first and crucial battle has been fought and won. D-day has taken place; but V-day awaits the second coming of Christ.[3] Then and then only will evil be finally destroyed.

The Scripture pictures this final destruction of Satan in vivid terms. There is a lake of fire prepared for the devil and his angels (Matthew 25:41). At the end of Christ's reign, every enemy will be destroyed, and the devil will be cast into the lake of fire (Revelation 20:10). His final doom is sure, for he is already a defeated enemy.

In summary, the Scriptures teach that the second

---

[3] Oscar Cullmann in his excellent book *Christ and Time* has popularized this idea.

coming of Christ is the means by which God will accomplish the destruction of His enemies and the gathering of His people into the blessings of the kingdom of God. The kingdom of God implies that the salvation of the individual is never viewed in detachment from the salvation of the people of God. The kingdom of God is therefore the final goal of human history.

The seeming difference in the prophetic expectation in the Old and New Testaments is inherent in progressive revelation. The Old Testament hope is expressed primarily in terms of the nation Israel as the people of God, while the New Testament further defines the people of God in terms of the Church. This New Testament redefinition does not, however, exclude Israel. Israel is yet to be saved and included in the people of God.

While there is a difference in emphasis, the underlying theology in the Old and New Testament hope is the same. In fact, the New Testament hope can be understood only in light of the Old Testament. The Old Testament looks forward to one great day of the Lord when evil will be destroyed and God's people gathered into His kingdom. The New Testament shows us that this goal of God's kingdom is to be achieved in two great redemptive acts. By His incarnation, life, death, and resurrection, Christ has entered into human history to attack the enemies of man and God. He has defeated the power of satanic evil, He has broken the dominion of death, He is gathering together a people in His Church who have been delivered from bondage to darkness and fear of death, who have experienced the power of His resurrection and shared His life. Yet evil and

44]

death continue; and although redeemed, even God's people still sin and die. We await the second coming of our victorious Lord to complete the conquest of our enemies and to bring us into the fullness of redemption. He who has already attacked and defeated Satan will come again to destroy him. He who came once to conquer death will come again to destroy it. When He comes again, He will gather His redeemed people into the kingdom of God, where they will be forever delivered from evil, sin, and death and will enjoy all that constitutes eternal life in fellowship with God.

V. The Second Coming and the Present Lordship of Christ

PETER COMFORTS believers experiencing fiery ordeals with the hope "that you may also rejoice and be glad when his glory is revealed" (I Peter 4:13). Paul also promises to suffering Christians the hope of rest "when the Lord Jesus is revealed from heaven" (II Thessalonians 1:7). The second coming of Christ will mean the *revelation*, the disclosure to the world, of the glory which already belongs to Him who is now the Lord in heaven.

The fact that the second coming of Christ will be the

[45

disclosure of His present lordship serves as a corrective to two unbiblical views of the kingdom of God. It corrects the view that God's kingdom can come apart from the second coming of Christ; it corrects the view that the kingdom of God belongs altogether to the future, without being at the same time one dimension of His present work. The coming of His kingdom will be the manifestation in the world of a reign which Christ entered at His resurrection and ascension. From one point of view, the return of Christ will import nothing new. It will disclose to the world the glory which He now possesses, manifest the lordship which He now enjoys, extend among men a reign He is now exercising.

The fact is that Jesus is now Lord. He is now enthroned at God's right hand as the messianic King. His second coming will display this lordship, acknowledged today only by believers, to all the world.

We have shown in the previous chapter that the kingdom of God means the effective, redemptive rule of Christ over His enemies. This conquest over His enemies—sin, death, and Satan—does not belong to the future only. By His life, death, and resurrection, Christ attacked and defeated Satan. He has already broken the power of death.

Now we are ready to consider a further fact: the ascension of Christ and His session or enthronement at the right hand of God is a further step in His conquest of evil. However, the victory which He won in His resurrection and ascension is now unseen by the world. As human history moves on, it sometimes seems as though Satan were the "god of this age" (II Corinthians 4:4)

46]

JESUS CHRIST AND HISTORY

in an almost unqualified sense of the word. However,
this is not true. It is only the appearance of things.
Back of the ebb and flow of history lies the fact that
evil has been defeated, Jesus has been enthroned as
Lord, and God is only waiting for His own hour until
Christ's lordship is revealed, evil is trampled beneath
His feet and His rule extended over the whole world.

In the temptation, Satan tried to turn Jesus away
from the cross by promising Him rule over the world
without suffering (Matthew 4:8–9). Yielding to this
temptation would have meant the victory of the rule of
Satan over the kingdom of God. Jesus faithfully and
unswervingly pursued the mission of obedience and
humility for which He had come. Although as the Son
of God He had existed with His Father in heaven in
the form of God, He had not seized upon equality with
His Father, but had emptied himself in humiliation by
taking the form of a slave and being born as a man
among men. As a man, He humbled himself yet further
and became obedient even to death on the cross. However, because of His obedience and faithfulness unto
death, God the Father has highly exalted Him. God
has raised Him from the dead, exalted Him to God's
own right hand, and bestowed upon Him the name that
is above every name: *Lord* (Philippians 2:6–11).

Jesus is *now* the Lord. This was the heart of the early
Christian confession: not Jesus as Savior, as is so often
true today, but Jesus as Lord. It is confession of Jesus
as Lord which saves (Romans 10:9). This was the sub-
stance of the early Christian gospel: Jesus Christ is
Lord (II Corinthians 4:5).

[47

This confession meant more than a personal relationship of total obedience to Christ, although obedience was included. It was first of all the confession of a theological fact. It meant the recognition that Christ actually *is* the Lord, enthroned in heaven. Because Jesus is the heavenly Lord, the individual believer submits to His lordship.

This was Peter's message on the day of Pentecost. The first Christian sermon proclaimed the fact of Jesus' lordship and appealed to men to accept it. Jesus, who had been crucified, could not possibly be left in the grave, for David had prophesied that God "would set one of his descendants upon his throne" (Acts 2:30). Peter finds proof of this in Psalms 110:1: " 'The Lord said to my Lord, Sit at my right hand, till I make thy enemies a stool for thy feet' " (Acts 2:34, 35). This Peter interpreted with the affirmation, "Let all the house of Israel therefore know assuredly that God has made him both Lord and Christ (Messiah), this Jesus whom you crucified" (vs. 36).

Lord and messianic King! This is Jesus' office even today. All authority has been given to Him in heaven and on earth (Matthew 28:18). He has been enthroned at God's right hand (Hebrews 1:3; 8:1; 10:12; 12:2). This fact signifies nothing less than that Jesus in His triumph and exaltation shares the very throne of God himself (Revelation 3:21). He is now reigning as King (I Corinthians 15:25); and He will continue His kingly reign until all His enemies have been made the footstool of His feet—until Satan and death are finally destroyed.

Now we can understand more precisely what the

second coming of Christ represents: the manifestation and the extension of His present reign over the world. The world does not know that He is now enthroned as Lord and King. Every knee does not bow and every tongue does not confess that He is Lord (Philippians 2:10–11). His lordship is indeed being proclaimed in all the world, but only those who accept the gospel confess His lordship and bow before His kingly rule. *This is why the second coming of Christ is absolutely necessary.* His return will be the means of bringing the struggle with evil to an end. The final victory is assured, because the initial victory has already been won, and He is already the victorious, regnant Lord and Christ.

This triumphant second coming of Christ is vividly pictured in the Revelation in terms of a conquering warrior (Revelation 19:11–16). The King of kings and Lord of lords, who is also the Word of God, is pictured as coming on a white battle charger. He is crowned with the insignia of royal power; His clothing is splashed with blood from the battle. He is accompanied by the armies of heaven, who are similarly garbed and mounted. However, the only weapon of conflict is a sword—a sharp sword issuing from the mouth of the returning King—the sword of His mouth, the Word of God.

What an incomprehensible conception! Who can take this picture *literally!* Who can conceive of a warrior with a sword swinging back and forth out of his mouth, chopping down his foes! Yet what a majestic conception! In the beginning, God spoke, and the world came into being (Genesis 1:9; John 1:1, 3; Hebrews 11:3). In

[49

the incarnation, God spoke, and redemption was accomplished (John 1:1–14; Hebrews 1:1–3). At the end, Christ will speak, and evil will be destroyed. However we are to understand the details, one central fact is sure. Christ will come; His kingdom will yet rule over all; every knee will bow and every tongue confess His lordship.

VI. The Second Coming and History

IN THE FIRST CHAPTER, we outlined several modern reinterpretations of history and eschatology which make little room for the second coming of Christ. One might ask, "If the teaching of the second coming is so very important in biblical thought, why do not all modern biblical interpreters accept it?"

The difficulty with this doctrine does not rest in the obscurity of the biblical teaching. It grows out of modern ideas about history. As we saw in the first chapter, the modern concept that history has destiny and purpose reflects the impact of the Old Testament idea of history moving to a divinely appointed goal. However, many of the modern interpretations have forsaken the biblical perspective at an all-important point. The Bible

50]

is God-centered, while our modern views are man-centered. History is no longer understood in a biblical sense but in a modernized sense. History is defined in terms of contemporary philosophies rather than in terms of God, the Lord of nature and history.

It is often said that if *history* really has a goal, this goal must be achieved within history and by historical forces. If history itself does not produce the kingdom of God, the kingdom is not really historical. Therefore we must seek to discover forces of progress and development within history. The idea of a heavenly Son of Man coming with glory from heaven does not mean the redemption of history. It means rather the destruction of history. Such concepts, we are told, are utterly foreign to historical experience. Rudolf Bultmann expresses it: "It is no longer possible for anyone seriously to hold the New Testament view of the world . . . We can no longer look for the return of the Son of Man on the clouds of heaven or hope that the faithful will meet him in the air." Therefore the New Testament notions about a heavenly Son of Man coming in glory cannot be an essential part of the gospel, but only the religious framework taken over by the early Christians from their environment of Jewish apocalyptic thought.

This is why Bultmann reinterprets eschatology altogether in terms of personal existence and confesses complete ignorance as to the goal of history. Such thinking, however, so radically reinterprets the gospel as to empty it of its fundamental character. For the gospel is not concerned alone with personal existence and individual salvation, although it includes these. The gospel con-

[51

sists of the redemptive acts of God in history; therefore it points to a goal for history as the final objective of God's redemptive acts. This is not to say that the final historical redemption is accomplished by history. Precisely here is the significance of the second coming of Christ: history cannot save itself. Evil is real. Evil is greater than man, greater than men, and stronger than all history. Only a mighty act of God breaking into history can save it.

This is the message of the whole Bible. This necessity for divine intervention to redeem history from the curse of sinfulness and evil is not limited to the second coming of Christ; it belongs to the entire redemptive line. The experiences of Israel in the Old Testament were the result of God's intervention. God was acting in history for Israel's blessing in a way He was not acting elsewhere in human affairs. Israel alone He called to be His people. Israel alone He delivered from bondage and led into the land of promise. To Israel alone, and to those who would come under Israel's influence, did He promise the kingdom of God. The fulfillment of these promises of the kingdom would not be the product of history, but would be the result of a divine act in history. God will arise and visit the earth in judgment and salvation. The divine visitation will bring judgment and salvation for both men and the world of nature. Out of the ruins of judgment will emerge both a new world, freed from the curse of evil, and a new people, cleansed from their sins and renewed in their hearts.

We have seen that the New Testament fulfillment of this Old Testament hope occurred in unexpected terms.

52]

Before the Son of Man comes in glory to bring the kingdom of God, He came as the suffering Servant, in weakness and humility to die. However, the New Testament clearly teaches that *both acts of the drama of redemption involve nothing less than an inbreaking of the world of God into human history.*

The life and death of Jesus of Nazareth was no mere "historical" event in the modern limited scientific sense of the word. Jesus was not, like Socrates or Epictetus, merely the product of a certain historical and religious environment. To be sure, Jesus appeared in a given historico-religious milieu of late Judaism, and He cannot be understood historically apart from this environment. However, one can master the environment and miss completely the significance of Jesus, for He was no less than God incarnate in the flesh. "In the beginning was the Word, and the Word was with God, and the Word was God . . . And the Word became flesh and dwelt among us" (John 1:1, 14). One of the most significant discoveries of modern gospel criticism is that the Jesus of the Synoptic Gospels is no less a portrait of a Divine Being than is the Jesus of the Fourth Gospel. The earliest Gospel relates "the gospel of Jesus Christ, the Son of God" (Mark 1:1).

Jesus of Nazareth was no mere product of history; He was the coming of God into history. In him God dwelt among men. In Him, the Eternal has invaded the temporal. In Him, the Absolute is known in the relativities of history. The virgin birth of Jesus does not stand apart as an irrelevant legend; it is of a piece with all that Jesus was and did. The virgin birth denotes nothing less

[53

than that Jesus of Nazareth was not the product of history. Only by a creative act of the eternal God, an act
quite inexplicable by all the physical sciences, did Jesus
come into the world. The virgin birth indicates that in
the coming of Jesus, something happened which transcends all historical causality and analogy. The pre-
existent Son of God "emptied Himself, taking the form
of a servant, being born in the likeness of men" (Philippians 2:7).

The resurrection of Christ is of a piece with His birth.
No mere reanimation of a corpse, it brought into view
the emergence of a new order of life in human history
—resurrection life—the life of the age to come. This
was such life as history had never before experienced
and could not of itself produce. There is not nor can
there be any natural "historical" explanation or analogy
of the resurrection. It is suprahistorical. It is a direct
unmediated act of God.

This act does not imply a breaking of the "laws of
nature." It indicates rather that God, the Creator and
Lord of nature, is not bound by His own creation, but
can act in nature by powers which exceed ordinary
human observation. The essential question is this: Are
human history and nature the measure of God and of
God's working? The biblical answer is an unequivocal,
No. While both man and nature are God's creation,
both are marred by sin; and only by an *intervention*
of God can either be redeemed. Left to itself, human
existence ends in death, and nature groans endlessly
under the burden of violence and corruption. The gospel is the good news that God has abandoned neither

man nor the world, but that He has intervened in the
miraculous birth, the miraculous life, and the miraculous resurrection of the incarnate Son of God. Even the
death of Christ involves a supernatural event, although
one that was entirely unseen. For in that awful death,
a spiritual event was taking place. Atonement was being made for the sins of men.

The incarnation of Christ and His second coming
alike are both interventions of God in human history.
He who has no room in his thinking for the second
coming of Christ, because it is not an "historical" event,
or because it is not consistent with historical experience,
does not really understand the biblical doctrine of incarnation. Incarnation represents an invasion into human history of the suprahistorical realm to accomplish
for man in history what man could not accomplish for
himself. The import of the second coming of Christ is
similar, but with this difference. The glory of the incarnate Son was veiled; the glory of the returning Son
will be manifest. No real contradiction to this statement
is found in John's statement, "We have beheld his glory,
glory as of the only Son from the Father" (John 1:14);
for the glory to which John refers was not an unveiled
glory but a concealed glory, evident only to the eye of
faith. Jesus first "manifested his glory" at Cana of Gali-
lee when He changed the water into wine (John 2:11),
but this glory was seen only by His disciples who believed on Him. All that others experienced at Cana was
unusually good wine. God's glory was there, but in a
hidden form, seen only by faith.

When Christ comes again, His glory will be unveiled,

displayed to the world. He will come "on the clouds of heaven with power and great glory" (Matthew 24:30). "He will sit on His glorious throne" (Matthew 25:31). He who came once to Bethlehem, to be greeted only by a handful of shepherds, will return to be seen by all. But in both incarnation and second advent, the same Lord comes from heaven to earth for man's redemption.

Therefore in a real sense, the coming of the kingdom of God means both the redemption of history and the end of history. It is not incorrect to think of the kingdom of God as a realm "beyond history," if by this we imply that the kingdom of God will involve an order of human existence transcending all past historical experience. It will be life in time and space on the earth; yet it will be life of a new and different order, for it will be human earthly existence lifted out of its present weakness, decay, strife, and death.

This fact is evident even in the Old Testament hope of redemption. "The lion shall eat straw like the ox" (Isaiah 11:7). How are these words to be interpreted? Are we to think of carnivorous animals with the teeth and digestive organs of cattle? The Scripture obviously does not ask such questions. This statement means that nature will be freed from violence. The lion will no longer prey on the ox, but will become placid. This single statement suggests a complete transformation of nature that we can scarcely imagine. What will nature be like without the struggle for survival and the strong preying upon the weak? What will the world be like without the cycle of life and death? Obviously it will not be nature as we know it, but nature lifted to a new

56]

level of existence that surpasses the limits of all human experience.

The New Testament teaching of resurrection reflects the same kind of transformation. In the resurrection, they "neither marry nor are given in marriage, for they cannot die any more, because they are equal to angels" (Luke 20:35–36) in this fact: that there is no death and therefore no need of procreation and the marriage relationship. But when we reflect on these words, how can we, in terms of present experience, conceive of human existence without aging and dying, procreation, and the sexual relationship? From a biological point of view, the entire present human endeavor centers around the sexual function. Such words indicate that the life of the age to come will stand in continuity with present history but will be different—so different that we can scarcely conceive of it even in the imagination, let alone in terms of actual experience.

The rapture of the Church at the return of Christ is another element in this transition from present history to the life of the age to come. When Christ comes, "the dead in Christ will rise first; then we who are alive, who are left, shall be caught up together with them in the clouds to meet the Lord in the air; and so we shall always be with the Lord" (I Thessalonians 4:16–17). The word "rapture" comes from the Latin rendering of "caught up" (*rapiemur*). For the living, it is equivalent to the resurrection of the dead. The dead in Christ will be raised; the living in Christ will be caught up to meet the Lord. This designates the same transformation into resurrection life for both the dead and living

[57

saints. "We shall not all sleep [in death], but we shall all be changed" (I Corinthians 15:51). Both the dead and the living who have already known the resurrection life of Christ in history will experience the redemption of the body. "For this corruptible must put on incorruption, and this mortal must put on immortality" (I Corinthians 15:53, AV). The rapture of the Church is the event by which the saved who are alive at Christ's return are translated into the resurrection life without passing through death. It is the symbol of transition into a new order of life that transcends all present historical experience.

Yet not quite; for "Christ has been raised from the dead, the first fruits of those who have fallen asleep" (I Corinthians 15:20). We have already pointed out that the resurrection of Christ was an actual event occurring in history, and yet that it stands apart from all history, without historical causality and without historical analogy. It was not the reanimation of a dead corpse but the emergence of a new order of life, appearing in history, but going beyond all historical experience.

The Gospels record that the resurrection body of Jesus was a real body which could be seen, heard, and felt, yet that it was different. Jesus could go and come freely. He suddenly appeared among His disciples (John 20:19; Luke 24:36) and with equal suddenness disappeared (Luke 24:31). The Gospels relate this strange conduct without comment or embellishment as simple "historical" facts. The only adequate explanation is that the resurrection body of Jesus was a real

58]

body that moved, nevertheless, in a higher order of existence, exceeding the ordinary laws of space and motion. Does this not involve essentially the same issue as that of a world in which the lion eats straw like an ox, in which there is neither procreation nor dying? God has implanted in the heart of human history an event which will ultimately transform human historical experience in the immortality and redeemed resurrection life of the age to come. Christ's resurrection in history is the beginning of the eschatological resurrection at the last day.

Here is the fundamental meaning of the second coming of Christ for history. Man cannot redeem himself, nor can history produce the kingdom of God. Perverted by sin, man has lost his way. Burdened by evil, history of itself is doomed. Speaking as a purely "objective" historian, Bultmann rightly describes the search for meaning in history as meaningless. Such familiar names as Auschwitz and Dachau speak of the snarl of irrational and demonic threads in the warp and woof of history, which men cannot weave into a meaningful and purposeful pattern.

The gospel is the good news that God has abandoned neither man nor history. In the incarnation of Christ, God has invaded human history to defeat the forces of evil that man cannot conquer. In the second coming of Christ, God will again invade history to finish the redeeming work He has begun. Redemption from beginning to end is the work of God who transcends history. The return of Christ is the means by which redemption will be consummated. Even so come, Lord Jesus!

[59

SUGGESTED FURTHER READINGS

BOWMAN, JOHN WICK, *The Religion of Maturity*. New York: Abingdon-Cokesbury Press, 1948.

——, *Prophetic Realism and the Gospel*. Philadelphia: The Westminster Press, 1955. While these books are not primarily concerned with the second coming of Christ, they provide an exposition of the theology of "Prophetic Realism," which turns attention away from the return of Christ to center it upon the present working of God's kingdom "on the plane of history."

BULTMANN, RUDOLF, *Jesus Christ and Mythology*. New York: Charles Scribner's Sons, 1958.

——, *The Presence of Eternity*. New York: Harper & Bros., 1957. The former book provides an introduction to Bultmann's program of "demythologizing," and the latter is a positive exposition of Bultmann's attitude toward history.

CAIRNS, EARLE E., "Philosophy of History," in *Contemporary Evangelical Thought*, Carl F. H. Henry, ed.; Great Neck, N. Y.: Channel Press, 1957. An excellent brief survey of various philosophies of history.

CAMPBELL, RODERICK, *Israel and the New Covenant*. Philadelphia: Presbyterian and Reformed Pub. Co., 1954. A "postmillennial" study which includes the salvation and christianization of the world within the church's historical mission.

COLLINGWOOD, R. G., *The Idea of History*. New York: Oxford University Press, 1946. A survey of the history of historiography, together with an exposition of one of the most influential modern interpretations of history.

60]

CULLMANN, OSCAR, *Christ and Time.* Philadelphia: Westminster Press, 1950.

——, "The Return of Christ" in *The Early Church,* A. J. B. Higgins, ed.; Philadelphia: Westminster Press, 1956. A critical European scholar defends the view that redemptive history must have an eschatological goal.

DODD, CHARLES HAROLD, *The Parables of the Kingdom.* New York: Charles Scribner's Sons, 1958.

——, *The Apostolic Preaching and its Developments.* New York: Harper & Bros., 1960.

——, *The Coming of Christ.* Cambridge: The University Press, 1951. The first book deals with the teachings of Jesus and contains Dodd's "symbolic" interpretation of apocalyptic language. The second book gives Dodd's defense of "realized eschatology." The third book is his most recent interpretation of the second coming of Christ.

LADD, GEORGE ELDON, *Crucial Questions about the Kingdom of God.* Grand Rapids: Eerdmans Pub. Co., 1952.

——, *The Gospel of the Kingdom.* Grand Rapids: Erdmans Pub. Co., 1959. These two books offer an interpretation of the kingdom of God both as God's redemptive acts in history and the eschatological goal of history.

——, "The Saving Acts of God," in *Basic Christian Doctrines,* C. F. H. Henry, ed.; New York: Holt, Rinehart, and Winston, 1962. A brief statement of the biblical concept of revelation in redemptive history.

MCINTYRE, JOHN, *The Christian Doctrine of History.* Grand Rapids: Wm. B. Eerdmans Pub. Co., 1957. The theme is discussed from a more philosophical perspective than the present essay.

ROBERTS, T. A., *History and Christian Apologetic.* London: Society for the Promotion of Christian Knowledge, 1960.

An excellent essay pointing up the limitations of a strict historical method in interpreting Christian origins.

SUMMERS, RAY, *The Life Beyond*. Nashville: Broadman Press, 1959. A comprehensive study of biblical eschatology from a conservative amillennial viewpoint.

WALVOORD, JOHN, *The Millennial Kingdom*. Findlay, Ohio: Dunham Pub. Co., 1959. A detailed defense of the dispensational interpretation.